On the Write Path - Poems from the Heart

Abbi Jinks

ISBN: 978-1-3999-5459-4

This book is dedicated to everyone on the journey into self healing and the inner work. Over the past few years I've been lucky enough to meet and work with some brilliant people who have helped me to question my beliefs, get clear on my vision, and discover my inner voice.

I've trained in the beautiful practice of transformational coaching and healed more of my past wounds than I even knew I had.
I am grateful to have reignited my love for DANCING and WRITING which have been hugely pivotal in my healing journey.

I have let go of many habits and patterns that were holding me back and now I'm writing and sharing my transformational poems and loving the journey! I continue to work with others, helping them to live their most fulfilling and empowered lives.
Thank you for buying this book, supporting my work and please remember....

You Are
Amazing

Acknowledgements

I would love to thank so many people for being part of this journey, inspiring me, suggesting topics, commenting on my poems, sharing my posts, supporting my crowd funder to publish the book, and BELIEVING IN ME!

Here are some of them:

Mandy Abbott, Judy Abdullah, Jackie Allin, Kezzabelle Ambler, Danïelle Andrews, Liz Ash, Laura Baker, Lee Baker, Andy Bailey, Tanya Bailey, Jane Bateman, Bex Bee, Marianne Berghuis, Michelle Bilson, John Blake, Kat Butterfield Delaney, Caroline Bobby, Kate Brown, Andrew Casselton, Roy Castleman, Wendy Caunce, Jane Christine, Gilly Clark, Amy Clarkson, Zoë Cobb, Tara Clabecq-Bristow, Julie Dore, Stephanie Duncan, Teri Dunstan, Jenny Ellson, Barbara Emery, Dina Ganatra, Ahimsa Grace, Lhamo Grace, Kelly Hall, Jane Hargreaves, Dawn Hickson, Margy Hodges, Kemal Hussein for being the best.
Susie Jamieson, Edward Jinks, Sandra Jinks, Ezgi Jinks-Hussein, Zeki Jinks-Hussein, Chris Jones, Emma Jupp, Amelia Kennard, Geoff King, Fuggo King, Sergey Kochergan, Fay Lakin, Gayatri Lawrence, Bevelee Leask, Gabriella Lovelock, Ben Lowrey, Sarah Madigan, Paula Malson, Emma Maxwell, Luke McGrath, Sarah McNeill, Georgina McMahon, Genevieve McMahon, Mike McMullins, Alana Melody, Jo Morris, Pippa Moss, Jason Munnelly, Dee Naughton, Vanina Oliveira, Ruth Osman, Roger Orysiak-Marrison, Amelia Pace, Lydia Percival, Catherine Pilkington, Kevin Pinel, Anne Prestwick, Marie Prince, Estella Ramos, Lewis Read, Aimee Rose, Rose Rouse, Abigail Schischa, Bettina Schluep Adams, Lynsey Scotland, Penny Shutt, Vaibhav Sinha, Lisa Smith, Kary Stewart, Patricia Teixeira, Georgina Thompson, Trish Turner, Bronwyn Tutty, Gay Wagstaff, Louisa Waite, Peter Wallis, Jan Warnes, Emma Williamson, MP Yamfam.

The band Mitakuye Oyasin for hosting my pivotal performance at Back To The Roots in 2022.
And the band The Levellers for inspiring me from a young age to speak my truth and speak up for what I believe in.

Contents

Welcome

Hello! and welcome to my book, of poetry and rhyme,
I hope that while you're here you have the most amazing time.

Day one and it's just begun,
I'm already having so much fun.
Of course there's a bit of pressure there,
But I'm telling myself I just don't care.
The words that come will be perfect I'm sure,
I'm good enough. I don't need to be more.
Trusting myself is my lesson in this,
It's paving the way to my absolute BLISS!
I hope you enjoy this journey with me,
And I hope that you feel inspired and free.
I hope your heart warms as you read these pages,
And you keep coming back to them, through the ages.

I know that for me, my mission to write,
Feels deep in my soul, absolutely right.
It feels like it's my channel to help if I can,
To anyone that needs it, to help build the clan,
The tribe, the community, the village of today,
Where we can share together, to work, rest and play.
I feel that it's needed, the time is now,
To share all our skills, together somehow.

This book is my gift to those who are ready,
Let's connect all together, grounded and steady,
To build a new way, to let go of the past,
Forgive ourselves and the system, let's move on, and fast!
Let's remind ourselves of our true inner power,
And let's blossom, each one of us, like a beautiful flower.

SOUL PURPOSE

I'm grateful that I'm writing this,
it's 6am, it's dark,
And these words are swimming round my head,
searching for a place to park.

I thought I could press snooze,
and get a bit more sleep,
But these words were literally calling me,
to get up with a leap!
When I make space to sit down and write,
it's like I have no choice,
The words keep coming, spilling out,
giving credence to my voice.

Some might call it a 'Soul Purpose',
others a 'Zone of Genius,'
For me it feels like it's a part of us,
that's somehow meant to free us.
It frees us from the boring stuff,
the 'should-do's', the mundane,
It guides us and encourages us
to go against the grain.

Because let's face it, no-one's purpose,
is to be working for 'the man,'
Sat at a screen, never feeling fulfilled,
despite doing the best you can.

So how do we know what our purpose is?
Our calling, or our dharma?
Sometimes we need to sit still and ask,
what makes us feel alive, and calmer?

What brings within you, that excitement and joy,
where time just passes on by?
What gives you the feeling of serenity,
like watching clouds move in the sky?
What have you always LOVED to do?
What gives you the biggest thrill?
Is there something you're so good at,
that it feels like a natural skill?

You've somehow assumed that because it's easy for you,
that others can do it as well,
So you've not allowed the space to cultivate it,
to really let your ability swell.
Sometimes for me when I sit down and write,
I feel like such a fraud,
It seems so weird then, when people cheer along,
and agree and even, applaud.

You see they're all different words,
but I feel like I'm cheating,
I'm just putting down lines to the same pattern,
repeating.
It just comes from nowhere,
I don't really have to think,
And it comes really fast,
like I'm always on the brink,

Of words coming through me
so thick and so fast,
I wonder how long
it is going to last.
But what is our purpose?

It’s the inner work, our healing.
It’s daring to love ourselves
and smashing through the ceiling,
Of limiting beliefs, stories,
and patterns that keep us stuck,
It’s about letting our light shine,
and trusting in more than just luck.

And when it gets tough,
we need to keep going,
Peeling off layers, getting deep,
and take opportunities that are flowing.
For years people said
'when you find the thing you’re meant to do,
the doors will open really fast',
but I couldn’t quite believe that to be true.

Please don’t use up your energy
on doing what other people think,
Remember they might already,
have let their own passions sink.
Be true to yourself,
and if that feels scary, go get help,
Go sit on the beach,
surrounded by kelp.

Go dance yourself silly,
get out of your head,
Go pottering in the garden
or make a sculpture in the shed.
Give yourself the opportunities,
try the things that bring you JOY!

Allow yourself to buy
that new gadget, or toy.
Get playful with your time,
get curious, go have fun,
Remember that at this time on earth,
you have only one...
Life to live, so LIVE it!
It doesn't have to be so hard,
Imagine that you've just been dealt,
the best ever winning card.

Listen to the callings
from deep within your soul,
And share your passions and your skills,
to let your life feel whole.

I think my soul purpose is actually,
really to keep on learning,
To love myself, to heal my triggers,
and to keep the pages turning.

FEELING LOST

I wonder if the swallows,
or the swifts start feeling doubt,
As they travel southwards every year,
no map to figure it out.
I wonder if the mole,
ever gets into a fuddle,
With all those paths it digs,
what a dark, confusing muddle.

I guess there are many ways,
in which we might feel lost,
Physically, emotionally,
or financially at a cost.
It can cause us stress to feel,
like we're not on the right track,
We might question whether to go forward,
or, should we be turning back?
We might not know the next step,
or even the direction,
We might feel unable to move,
stuck, fearful of rejection.

I guess for me feeling lost,
is like a blip in intuition,
There's something getting in the way,
stopping ideas coming to fruition.
There may be interference,
from many other sources,
We may be at a crossroads,
with strong opposing forces.
We might feel it's too hard to choose,
we're scared of getting it wrong,

Like there's one correct way,
and if we screw up now, the implications will last too long.
I wonder how we can ALLOW feeling lost,
just let go and surrender,
Like back in the day, waking up somewhere new,
after being on a massive bender.

Trust is the key, right?
To making it safely home,
Knowing you'll eventually find your way,
forever you won't roam.
How can you invite that in now,
the surrender and the trust?
And come back to your inner guidance,
so you're not feeling fussed?

How can you embrace the feeling
like a spider drifting on its web?
How can you allow yourself to move,
gently with the flow and the ebb?
Of each day and each moment,
each season in life,
From Falmouth to London,
or even up to Fife!

I guess some would say that you'll never feel lost,
if your anchor is rooted within,
And you'll know in your heart that each day brings a
chance,
to start over again and begin.
What if feeling lost is the springboard to climb,
To propel you to new heights where you'll feel sublime?

Where your skills are rewarded,
your nervous system is soothed,
Where you're no longer fearing
the wrath of the sabre-toothed,
Creatures of our past,
who our ancestors ran from,
What if your next phase in life
is to feel absolute FREEDOM?

So allow feeling lost,
it's part of the journey,
And know it will pass,
like all the other types of worry.
You're safe to feel lost,
and to feel found,
Just keep feeling your body
supported by the ground.
Feel the support and the love
surrounding you now,
I promise it's there,
even if you can't feel it somehow.

If you lean into trust,
and love and support,
You'll let go of oppressive stories
you may have been taught.
Where success and abundance
are only meant for the few,
That's not true,
there's plenty out there for me and for you.
As with most things in life
that are clouding our vision,
My first suggestion would be
to turn off the television!

Get rid of the news
and the stories of woe,
Clear out all the substances
that keep you feeling slow.
If you can do that,
and really be true,
To yourself and your wisdom,
well, there's no stopping you!

CHOICE

I want to shout this from the rooftops,
so you can hear my voice,
I'm here to remind you,
that you, have a choice.
Every single moment,
every single day,
Even when it doesn't really
seem that way.

It can be hard to accept,
that you have the power to choose,
Such a massive concept,
it can feel safer to stick with the blues.
It might feel easier
to say that you can't,
Or to blame other people,
or to say that you just aren't,
Able to do things differently,
permitted to say 'Thanks but no,
I'll make my own mind up on this one',
after all, who's running the show?

Is it my friends or family,
society or the government?
Is it someone outside of me,
saying for me what is meant?
Do you find yourself going along with the majority,
just because that's what they're doing?
Or do you readily question tradition and rules?
Do you have your own ideas brewing?

I hear so many people,
say they couldn't possibly leave their job,

Then they get home every single night
and sit on their sofa, and sob.
I know friends who put up with relationships
that are detrimental to their health,
And others who resign themselves to the 'fact',
that they'll never enjoy any wealth.

How many of us let fear take over,
and basically do what we're told?
Without even checking in for ourselves,
if it's the best idea we're being sold.
I know it can feel scary,
I'm not saying it will be easy,
For me when I've done something different,
I'm often left feeling queasy.

It can feel unsafe in our bodies,
to go against the herd,
We somehow believe we must act for the group,
our boundaries get all blurred.
It's our subconscious mind, trying to keep us alive,
it's what it's supposed to do,
It wants us to be like the others in the tribe,
so if they survive, we do too.

That subconscious mind has been working real hard,
since even before we were born,
It takes in 11 million bits of information per second,
and, you might not like this next bit, I warn:

You don't have control over your subconscious mind!
And it's had years of being programmed,

Ideas and theories, beliefs and fears,
into your brain have been repeatedly rammed.

Now that's not all bad, of course!
It works great,
To keep us alive,
but do you want it to dictate,
How you live out your life?
Your health, your career?
How much money you have?
Your formation of ideas?

The thing is it's working all of the time,
It's probably why I can't stop writing in rhyme!
'Cos for years I read stories to my kids in their bed,
And the rhythms and rhymes then got stuck in my head.

You might think
'oh well, that's a small bit of my mind'
But actually it's most of it,
95%, and it's blind,
To the difference
between what's false and what's reality,
It looks for repeated patterns
and it loves familiarity.

So if you're watching programmes
where people are fat,
Your subconscious mind works
to recreate just that.
If you're giving up alcohol
then watch any Hollywood film,
You'll find it hard to stop,
because the producers are at the helm.

What I'm saying right here with the subconscious stuff,
is that it affects all our decisions,
So it is important to check in with what we witness,
in life, or on televisions.

I made the choice a long time ago now,
to switch off that box in the corner,
I want to live my very best life,
and no longer feel like the mourner,
To a life I don't love where I'm making myself ill,
doing things that really don't serve me.
I know I have a choice to reprogramme my brain,
to help me feel more and more free.

So I can choose what I watch,
and my circle of friends,
But what about this victimhood
that feels like it never ends?

What about this feeling
of being stuck in a situation?
Well just reminding myself that it IS a choice,
might lead to anticipation,
Of other ideas, of alternatives,
where I no longer have to feel coy,
I can trust in myself to make more decisions
that will welcome in a bit more JOY!

When you realise that you have a choice,
often things then start to feel,
Easier somehow, less of a grind,
no longer is life an ordeal.

You can choose how to react,
you can choose to change,
You can choose to get help,
and to rearrange,
The thoughts in your head,
the patterns, the beliefs,
And my goodness that realisation,
can bring such a relief.

Please remember your power,
come what may,
You always have a choice,
every single day.

INTUITION AND BELIEF

It's a really simple message this one,
knowing it can bring relief,
It's all about a couple of words,
INTUITION, and BELIEF.
There are so many things
you can believe in this world,
Many, many theories,
with evidence unfurled.

There are laws of science,
rules of thumb,
Your Dad says it's one thing,
'no it's the other' says your Mum.
There are people claiming
their way's best,
'just listen to me,
forget the rest.'

There are doubters and haters
and critics all around.
There are those who say
life's answers will never be found.
There are some who say,
'you'll never make it, you should have studied harder,'
There are some who say,
'the end is coming, have a well stocked larder.'

There are some who say there's a set of rules,
and following them, will bring success,
There are others who say that following rules,
is what made all the mess.

There are systems and structures
and guidelines in place,
Some of them fair,
some to keep you in the race.

So who do you listen to?
What do you follow?
The truth of that answer
can be hard to swallow.
Because really and truly,
you're the only one to know,
Which path at every crossroads
is the way for you to go.

You're the only one living
your life right now,
Nobody else
can show you how.
To live it, to breathe it,
which chances you should take.
And the best thing to do
when you've got a decision to make...

...is to listen to your body,
your heart, your gut,
Knowing some doors will open,
and some, will shut.
And believe me that's ok you know.
It really is,
When you trust and believe,
you won't get in a tis.

You won't worry what you're missing,
or what everyone else is doing,
You'll be so tuned in, to your own path,
the 'right' answers will be ensuing.
Your intuition holds a blueprint,
written just for you,
And if you allow it to speak,
it will tell you what to do.

Your intuition can guide you,
it can really light the path,
And if you follow it with love,
you can let go of the aftermath.
If you trust and believe in yourself,
every day,
You'll find that living out your life
becomes a bit like play.
You're playing with the options,
weighing up ideas,
You're tuning in, to what feels good,
and not to all your fears.

But what is intuition?
To those who do not know,
It's that part of you that at the top of a cliff,
screams loudly 'NO!'
It's the part of you that rings your child
when you have a hunch or feeling,
And you hear them tell a story,
of the friend they just caught stealing.

It's when someone asks if you'd like to join them
on an outing or a trip,

And you can't decide so you toss a coin,
but ignore the answer from the flip.
And something goes wrong
and you know deep inside,
That you weren't meant to be there,
it wasn't your ride.

So there's two things right here:
there's the internal knowing,
And then there's the ideas,
that keep on flowing.
Which ones do you go for?
Which do you choose to believe?
Which are the good ones
and which ones deceive?

So the best way to describe it
is to tune into your body,
Learn to pay attention to what's feeling off,
or shoddy.
It will come with practice
and over time,
You'll be making decisions quicker
than tossing a dime.

You need to get into your body
and out of your head,
Set aside all your worries
about finances in the red.
Leave at the door,
any past regrets,
And don't allow your future
to be taken over by frets.

You could try to meditate daily,
being still and quiet,
Allow your mind to be present,
not fixed on someone else's riot.
You can cut out the things
that take you out of yourself,
Leave the uppers and downers,
high up on the shelf.

Well anyway what I'm saying is,
to cut to the core
When you're there in your heart,
there's a belief you can't ignore,
There's a truth deep inside you
that's burning hot and bright,
When you really can feel it,
all your answers are in sight.

Let messages come to you,
let them nudge and guide you,
Then all you've got to do
is let 'BELIEF' override you.
Not doubt, or fear.
Or someone else's nay say,
Your belief in yourself
is what counts on the day.

You want to be an athlete?
A champion of your game?
Then make space for belief in you
and let go of any shame.
Whatever it is you want in life,

whatever is there in your soul,
To make it happen, belief is the key,
to get the ball starting to roll.

You've got to believe it's possible,
you've got to believe you can,
You've got to become your number one
and most supportive fan.
You've got to trust it will happen for you,
without yet knowing the way,
You've got to believe you can, simple.
Every. Single. Day.

RESISTANCE

Resistance! Hello!
Dear friend of mine,
Thank you for your help
but I'm actually fine.
Please don't get involved,
please just let me be,
I actually want to write this morning,
can't you see?

I know that pile of washing
needs hanging out,
And I've a really long to-do list,
of that there is no doubt.
And I'm sure if I just checked
that other book said,
My writing would come across
as if I'm 'better read'.

But you see if I stop and listen to you,
There's a danger I won't ever,
actually see the thing through.
I won't ever push past
the invisible wall,
That you've built so meticulously
to keep me feeling small.

Sorry, I know you'd say
you've built it to keep me safe,
To protect me from what's out there,
you see me as a waif,
Someone frail and tiny,
and weak I guess,

You're protecting me
from ever getting into a mess.

And I thank you for that,
I really do,
You and my subconscious,
have it all thought through.
You have it all worked out,
and your stories are convincing,
And I know that with your words,
you are never one for mincing.

You tell me I might fail,
and that would probably hurt,
You remind me I could fall
and land with my face in the dirt.
You tell me that I'm tired
so back to bed I should go,
You tell me that it's just too hard,
it'll only end in woe.

You question who I think I am
to try to do something different,
'It's pointless' you say, futile even,
to go against the current.
Much better just to stay right here,
safely, stay the same,
You say 'no-one ever got happy, really,
through riches, and fame.'

Do I think I'm special?
Who do I think I am?

I might as well give up now,
this opportunity might be a scam.
'It's really very scary out there,'
you tell me every day,
Why bother sharing my vulnerable self,
just imagine what they'll say.

They might laugh at me, ignore me,
they might think I'm full of it,
They might judge me as not good enough,
so you tell me it's not worth it.
It's a bit like when I want to go for a run,
or to a fitness class,
Resistance does a really good job
of trying to keep me on my arse.

It tells me it's too cold out there,
makes out like it's protecting my health,
And it does that in the most covert ways,
it's amazing at being stealth.
It really is creative,
in coming up with reasons,
To not let me, do, the, thing.
It has some for all the seasons.

The thing that can help,
turn resistance into a teacher,
Is to notice it's there,
see it as a shape shifting creature.
It will come back,
with many, different disguises,
It might lovingly create,
some distracting surprises.

It might tell you that you,
don't belong, here, right now,
And you might take its word for it,
and from this moment, vow,
To never even go there,
to not even try,
You might convince yourself that you,
don't even know why,
You're doing the thing anyway,
what was the actual plan?
So the trick to combating resistance
is to keep saying 'I CAN.'

I can do the thing,
it's important to me,
These steps that I'm taking,
they help me to feel free,

Or happy, or healthy,
or wealthy one day.
Getting in touch with your reason 'why'
will help you to slay,
The monster that is resistance,
that clever, little beast,
Or maybe you could tame it
and bring it along to the feast.

The feast that will be bestowed on you,
the other side of the line,
The line that you must cross every day,
to allow yourself to shine.
When resistance really puts up a fight,

that's a sign to push on through,
Because beyond that, you'll often find,
the most powerful step for you.

So keep going, always,
keep showing up, please,
Even when it feels like
it's a bit of a squeeze.
Because just like the caterpillar,
that leaves the cocoon,
If it didn't squeeze through a tiny hole,
its wings would never bloom.

If a seed doesn't get covered
in damp, dark mud,
It would never get a chance to sprout,
let alone to bud.
So believe me when I tell you,
that what is stopping you,
Is a massive pile of resistance,
all sticky like glue.

It's job is to push you back
and test your resolve,
So wave your wand of BELIEF everyday
and let resistance, dissolve.

MOTHERHOOD

So let me tell you,
about being a mother.
Essentially it's caring,
for, another.
They start off helpless
and needing you,
To feed and clothe,
and clean up poo!

Then as they grew,
I started to see,
Just how much of them,
is a reflection of me.
When my son was born,
I had no idea,
That what would ensue,
would raise heaps of fear.

Am I getting it wrong?
Is everyone else doing better?
Why won't he sleep?
I'm following advice to the letter.
I stressed and worried,
and looked outside,
Of myself for the answers,
to this brand new guide.

I didn't realise I,
should be following him,
And trusting myself,
to deal with every whim.
It brought up in me,

a whole host of stories,
No, not the fairy tales
or jack-a-nories.

Those beliefs and ideas
that were stored in my head,
They were rising up now
to allow me to shed,
The layers, the barriers,
the BS, and blocks
It was like having a kid,
could get me out of the box.

The box I'd created,
out of fear, shame and shoulds,
For me, I had a new light,
leading me out of the woods.
What I see in my child
as less than enough,
Is really my own self,
where the love I have is tough.
Where for years I've been critical
and ignored my own needs,
Like a child crying out
for a comforting feed.

For me, being a mother,
is really a way,
Of parenting myself,
in a more gentle way.
It's time to care
for my own inner child,

The one who needs healing
and is too scared to smile.

To all the mums out there,
you really rock!
It's hard and it's full of questions like,
'where's my sock?!'
It can feel overwhelming
when the load is with you,
But we weren't meant to do it alone,
that ain't true.

We've always been held
and supported by others,
With friends, Nans and sisters,
not just the mothers.
So let's rebuild the village,
one built to care,
And get back in community
to cook, play and share!

THIS TOO SHALL PASS

One thing I've learned,
that I think it's worth to share,
From this life lived so far,
lessons appearing everywhere,
Is that feelings are our guides,
like clues in the game,
They hold messages and pointers
towards prizes we can claim.

So if we're feeling happy,
we know our needs are being met,
We might feel full, safe, connected,
nothing's causing us to fret.
But if we're feeling angry,
or sad or depressed,
We might start to question things,
'why aren't I being blessed?'

We go straight into wanting,
to fix those sensations,
We make ourselves wrong,
we blame our very foundations.
We can sometimes ignore them
and push them aside,
But what we resist persists my friend,
there is nowhere to hide.

If you're sad, go seek comfort,
that is what you need.
Just like when you were little
and a grazed knee began to bleed.

If you're angry, feel the anger,
it's probably because,
Somewhere around you,
a boundary has been crossed.

Every single feeling, is perfectly OK,
Sometimes we feel hundreds
on any given day.
And before you begin to analyse
and write stories in your head,
Just remember that feelings aren't meant to be thought,
they're meant to be FELT, instead.

So stop and feel them in your body,
let all of them bubble up,
Acknowledge what's going on and allow it,
then remember to fill your cup,
With what you NEED on a regular basis,
tune in with what feels good,
Do you need to create, to let off steam,
or a quiet walk in the wood?

Allow your feelings to guide you,
let them light the path,
And remember no matter how good,
or uncomfortable it is, always 'this too shall pass.'

It helped me out so much that phrase,
when I became a mum,
Things felt hard and different
and I sometimes wanted to run!
But each day and night and tricky phase,

as well as all the joy,
DID pass and move, to the next one,
just like each early toy.
And the same with all of us you know,
remember to hold on tight,
And allow each feeling to come and go,
just as day turns into night.

If feelings stay stuck
or move up to your head,
I'd recommend dancing,
rather than going to bed.
And if you have wobbles
and fall on your arse,
Remember again,
THIS TOO SHALL PASS!

MENSTRUATION

This one's about
the monthly bleed,
I'm a bit lost for words,
I must concede.
I guess it's from years
of keeping it quiet,
That somehow this topic
is not in our verbal diet.

Years and years
of being too scared to say
'Actually I'm bleeding,
I need to rest today'
As women we've often
just been told to get on,
With the day to day tasks
as if nothing was wrong.

And nothing IS wrong,
that's a whole other myth,
It's a perfectly natural
part of life, to live with.
The truth is each month,
women need to slow down,
To listen to their bodies,
not push on with a frown.

We need to respect
our time to release,
And feel safe and supported
to lay down in peace.
We also need,
to be able to share,

Other womanly things,
like, body hair!

There's so much in secret,
shrouded in shame,
We make ourselves wrong,
and feel we're to blame.
Well not any longer,
let's speak our truth!
Let's wave our red flags
at the top of the roof.

Let's show young girls
we're not creating a fuss,
We are women, and warriors
and it's great to be us.
We have incredible bodies,
that can grow new life,
Let's celebrate that,
making red tents rife.

Through the country, the city,
our homes and our schools
Let's be celebrating women
and breaking old rules.
And let's tell our brothers,
our uncles and our dads,
That we're changing each month,
not going through fads.

We need help from our men,
their love and support,

And sometimes, we even,
need battles to be fought.

Yes we are strong
and we can do things alone,
But when truly supported,
our real creativity is grown.

So with every woman
across the nation,
Let's celebrate our
MENSTRUATION!!

NATURE

One, two, three, four,
Breathe in, breathe out, breathe more.
Listen to the rhythm, feel the beat,
Connect with the ground beneath your feet.

Feel the air fill up each lung,
Taste the rain upon your tongue.
Listen to the waves, crashing and breaking,
Nature is REAL, there is no faking.

Sit, stand, be still and hear,
What's it whispering into your ear?
Nature is such an amazing teacher,
Just look at each tiny and detailed feature.

Feel the power, the wisdom, the strength,
It's all around you at an arm's length.
There are no mistakes, there's nothing to hide,
And that's why nature is such a guide.
It follows its own path, no overthinking,
When it's hungry it eats, if thirsty starts drinking.

When in the woods, I feel so calm,
It's like my own, nature balm.
I wonder why folk get stuck indoors,
And feel trapped and depressed, surrounded by laws,
When there's freedom and peace down a quiet track,
Go walking one day and don't look back.
Go get lost in the trees and smell the rich air,

Climb a mountain with friends, such a beauty to
share.

Pick a bramble and taste the perfection of flavour,
Then stare at the clouds, do yourself that favour.
Watch the morning sun, rise,
Enjoy each unfurling, coloured surprise.
Get up to hear birdsong, the dawn, chorus,
And imagine the orchestra creating it for us.
Go sit in a hammock under dappled shade,
Watch ants marching, on their parade.

Whittle a spoon from wood that you felled,
Then witness a storm while being safely held,
By a partner, a lover, a parent or child.
Then go jump puddles, go absolutely wild.
Smell all the roses EVERY time you walk by,
And notice the starlings as they fly,
In murmuration, moving as one,
Are they sharing food tips or is it just for fun?
How many beautiful spectacles to behold.
Just look at an amethyst or dig for GOLD!

Nature is here, and it's there,
Above you, below you, it's everywhere.
From the softest petal to the toughest grit,
Nature is within you, and you within it.

MANIFESTATION

Hmm, manifestation, I've been pondering this all week,
Essentially it's the art of creating what we speak.
Some call it a secret, it can feel elusive,
But it is for everyone, not at all exclusive.

The thing is we're doing it, all of the time,
As we daydream or worry, or watch TV shows full of
crime.
The Law of Attraction as it's also known,
Is about receiving the fruits of the seeds we have sown.

And those seeds are our thoughts, our visions, our words,
What we give our attention to, it's a bit like the birds,
Who migrate every summer, they don't know why,
It's just in their nature that they must fly.

And the same with the things that we want to come near,
It's a law of nature that they must appear.
When we are in tune with how good we'll feel,
It is then that the universe will make them real.

You see everything is made up of energy,
And everything has its own vibrating frequency.
We attract what we vibrate, whether joy, love or fear,
If that doesn't make sense, let me give you an
idea.

If you picture yourself on a warm sunny beach,
The feelings you imagine are what's within reach.
If you feel peaceful, relaxed and calm,
Then gradually things will appear, like a charm.

If you regularly feel anger, fear, guilt and shame,
You'll find yourself in situations creating more of the same.
If you notice you're moaning, complaining and critical,
You might have a bad day and think 'this is typical'.

However, if you're grateful for each part of your day,
The sunshine, fresh water, a moment to play,
You'll find that you see things in a whole new light,
And everything will come to you when the timing is right.

The trick, if there is one, is to let go of insistence,
Don't try to force things into existence.
The other thing that's key is to KNOW WHAT YOU WANT!
It may seem so simple but many focus on what they don't.

So a handy expression, I use to remind us,
Is the phrase, 'Hocus Pocus, where is your focus?'
When you notice your mind starting to stray,
Come back to the good feelings of the day.

And when you start imagining your visions and dreams,
Let go of the fact that it's not yet how it seems.

Don't get yourself stuck on the lack of that thing,
Just know and believe it's coming, then sing!
Sing songs of joy, love and gratitude,
Keep yourself in an appreciative attitude.

Keep on taking action, and let the universe do the rest,
Then be ready and be grateful as they all manifest.

DANCING

Have you ever been told,
you can't dance, you've no beat?
Or even you're too big,
you've got two left feet?
Well let me assure you,
whoever said that was wrong.
Every single body
can dance to their song.

In my 20s I danced
through the night at clubs,
Fuelled on drugs and drink
from dealers and pubs.
I would get quite literally
out of my head,
Keeping moving all night,
seldom seeing my bed.

It became an obsession,
a reason for being,
I felt so alive,
the movement was freeing.
But for so many years,
I gave all the credit,
To the pills and the powders,
I felt loved up, I said it,
Was due to THEM
that I felt so great,
They were raising me up,
causing my mood to elate.

I couldn't seem to go out,
without chemical assistance,

My beliefs on this were strong
and created much resistance
to dancing freely as I was,
sober and tired.
As with so many others,
it was just easier to get wired.

But not any more!
I've been doing the work,
As a mum I've responsibilities,
I cannot shirk.
The drugs went first,
that was actually pretty easy,
As I'd stopped going out,
no more parties all sleazy.

Then, the booze stopped,
though it put up a fight,
It kept saying 'go on try again,
this time you just might,
Be able to drink me,
to enjoy feeling drunk,'
But no, so much has changed,
drinking's firmly in the trunk.

But it left me a huge hole,
an emptiness to fill,
Was I actually fun without it?
Could life ever be a thrill?
Well that's where dancing comes
flying back into this story.
A few years ago, dancing returned,
saying 'please don't ignore me.'

It said 'get out of your head again'
but this time, not all lairy,
It meant 'get into your body,
I promise you it's not scary.'
And oh my gosh, can I tell you here,
how much dancing means to me?
If you want the secret to feeling good,
try dancing, it IS the key!

When you dance, you move, you flow through the air,
connect with how you're feeling,
That deep connection with yourself,
it's actually a spiritual healing.
Dance alone, dance together, wherever you are,
keep dancing and keep smiling,
And notice the thoughts and feelings come up,
start noting them down and filing,
The patterns, the stories, the worries you have,
be aware of all the insights.
Cos believe me when you're truly in flow,
they come through as the brightest lights.

It's like dancing is the key,
to open the door to your soul,
Every time I move my body to music,
I feel complete and whole.
And as for those folks
who told you you shouldn't,
Let's send them some love
for they too believed they couldn't.

It's time to break free
of those limiting beliefs,

Just get on that dance floor
where there are no chiefs.
No-one to tell you
what steps you should take,
Dancing's about FEELING,
so let's the rules break!

It's about feeling good in your body,
your mind and your soul,
And letting feelings move through you,
so shake, rattle and ROLL.
I invite you to step into
your life's biggest romance,
Take yourself to a space,
put the music on and DANCE!!!!

PERCEPTION

What do you see
as you gaze upon this earth?
Looking around,
do you have cause to feel mirth?
Do you see opportunity,
creativity and love?
Or do you see destruction
raining down from above?

Are you seeking
the positive aspects in people?
Or are you spotting cracks
on the way up the steeple?
We all see so differently,
through many a tinted lens,
What surrounds us makes an impact,
from the mountains to the fens.

We might have a conversation
with someone fresh and new,
And then start to ponder differently,
even change our point of view.
We might experience something painful,
a loss or deep felt grief,
And then start feeling more grateful,
notice the beauty in a leaf.

Butterflies have 12,000 eyes!
I mean, just imagine the world they see,
They must observe some detail,
that is hidden from you and me.
A kestrel sees in fluorescent light,

it's like another world,
If you've ever taken psychedelic drugs,
you probably had visuals to behold!

I once heard this great concept,
that there's no such thing as fact,
There are only opinions
and they can change,
depending
on the evidence stacked.
So before you believe what's presented to you,
the division and confusion,
Have a think about what's true for you,
and what might be illusion.

Does a bee become scary
just because it can sting?
Have you ever been told,
that you can't sing?
And what about that glass,
is it half full or half empty?
Is £100 enough?
Too much? Or plenty?

You see it all depends on how you frame it,
and which way your mind is set.
Do you tell yourself you've almost made it?
Or do you say, 'huh, we're not there yet?'
I guess for me, like most of life,
it comes back to intention,
If I look for how things are perfect,
that gives a shift to my attention.

Every obstacle becomes a challenge,
a choice of which way to go,
And it helps me see the lesson,
from which I can learn and grow.
One of my favourites to shift my mind,
and it really really works,
Is to swap out 'I HAVE to', and swap in 'I GET to',
and feel how my whole being smirks.

And sometimes, after doing something
with heartfelt connection,
My mind's really opened
and I've changed my perception.
The changing tides and seasons,
bring us deeper into our layers,
And if we perceive it so, life's a game,
where you and me are the players.

So perceive it's fun, believe you can,
do all the things that you dream,
And if you're feeling it's hard, believing you can't,
know that things aren't always as they seem!

COFFEE

To my dear old friend coffee,
I must write you this note.
I want to be clear about our break-up,
and I'm not here to gloat.
You served me so loyally
for many, many, years,
And I know since we parted
there might have been tears.

I don't know how it started,
I can't remember my first cup,
Maybe I was feeling tired,
and wanted to wake up.
Maybe someone else was having one,
and offered it to me,
Maybe everyone was having it,
and I thought it was meant to be?

I loved you for years,
hardly missing a day,
I thought you were great for me,
helped me to relax and play.
I craved the alertness,
that energised feeling,
Where I could chat on full speed
and bounce off the ceiling.

It was like when without you,
I wasn't quite myself,
Like you had my personality
somehow locked up on a shelf.
And the only way I,

could feel OK,
Was to drink at least one cup,
every single day.

But that sounds like addiction
and surely that can't be right,
So I wonder why so many folks
are caught up in the plight,
Of drinking a coffee
every morning without fail,
Could it be that without it,
they think that they might derail?
And perhaps they would to begin with,
giving up can feel hard,
I'm so grateful that I did it,
it's like I've been dealt a whole new card.

I FEEL LESS TIRED WITHOUT YOU COFFEE!
It's hard to believe I know,
You've cleverly persuaded us
you're essential to living 'on the go.'
But I've done some delving into your past,
in the time, since we split,
And basically, what I've learned
is that you are full of sh*t.

After drinking a cup,
blood flow to the brain is lower,
By up to half,
so my whole system is slower.
I'm getting half the nutrition
from anything I eat,
And also the waste products,

aren't able to excrete.
Coffee is a poison,
a natural pesticide,
The plant makes it to protect itself,
because it can't run and hide.
AND it's the most highly sprayed crop,
currently in production,
Just imagine those extra toxins,
causing my body, destruction.
Do you rely on coffee,
for your daily poo?
Have you ever stopped to question,
what it's actually doing to you?

Oh and just in case you're thinking,
'I just drink tea, I'm all right',
Anything with caffeine,
has the same effects, same bite.
It causes stress on your system,
activating fight, flight or fear,
That feeling of your heart pumping,
but where the threat is, you've no idea.

It actually makes sleep worse,
it interrupts your deep cycle of rest,
So you wake feeling groggy,
and can struggle to get yourself dressed.

It isn't good for your stomach,
as I've already said,
And without it, you get this incredible
pounding in your head.

Oh and did I mention it's addictive,
you just want more and more,
To get you back to feeling like yourself,
like you used to once before.

And what else have I learnt,
since I've been free of your grip?
You're another way of numbing pain.
Every time I felt a dip,
in mood, I could drink you
and block out all that yuck.
I could keep those feelings pushed down
and stay safe, or maybe stuck.
Stuck in the patterns of a life
that needed healing,
Who knew that what I needed
was to own all my feelings?

Coffee you're everywhere,
I commend you on your tries,
You're in cafes, shops, all over the place,
and in films as a subconscious surprise.
To keep me wanting more of you,
even though I've said 'No more,'
You keep getting in the programming,
now I see it, it's such a bore.

I wish you would give up your efforts,
and let me live in peace,
But it looks like you won't,
so my job now, is to help others to release,
You from their sacred lives too,

and to start feeling freer and clearer,
To help them get their visions set,
and bring them nearer and nearer.

Because although you're just a hot and dark,
steamy, bitter, drink,
When people consume you every day,
they are actually on the brink,
Of health issues so numerous
I won't list them here today,
But truly and simply,
what I'm here to say,
Is that coffee and caffeine, chocolate too,
they're not your friend,
And if you'd like to know more,
my ear is here for you to bend.

I know it's hard to hear these words,
if you're in the caffeine haze,
But believe me when you kick the habit,
you're destined for better days.

So coffee, to end this note of mine,
with love and gratitude I send you,
Off to your new adventures,
I'm no longer here to defend you.
So farewell to you, coffee
and your seductive temptation,
I'm off to help folk live their best lives
at their highest, vibration!!

SELF-LOVE

'So what is self-love?'
I hear you ask,
To really understand it
can be quite a task.
We know love for others,
of putting them first,
Now let's imagine you're perfect,
no better, no worse,
Than anyone else
here on this planet,
Not your mum or your brother,
your friends or Aunt Janet.
That's the first step I'd say,
to feeling self love,
It's to acknowledge we're all equals,
none below and none above.

Next it's talking to yourself in a way
that shows you care,
So I invite you right now,
hands on heart, let's declare:
'I am worthy. I am welcome.
I am enough as I am,'
Let those words sink in, repeat them,
every day if you can.

It can feel hard to say them,
I know it can feel tough,
There are so many ways
we've been told that we're not good enough.
But let me assure you,
reading this today,

You're ABSOLUTELY GOOD ENOUGH!
In your own special way.

So how do you get
to that place in your heart?
Where you feel really peaceful?
It is a bit of an art.
For me it started with checking in,
with exactly how I was feeling,
Sadness? Anger? Fear or Joy?
Was my body calm, or reeling?
Because for years
I'd never understood feelings at all,
I thought emotions were something
to throw at the wall,
To dismiss, push aside,
ignore at all costs,
I didn't see how they could help me
to not feel so lost.

So feelings came first,
followed by their handy companion,
I looked at my NEEDS,
which was an unchartered dominion.

Another new world,
I never knew that I had them,
But Oh My Goodness!
What a revelation now I've found them.
There's a whole list out there,
a list of every human need,
And understanding these

is like getting to know self-love, at speed.
You might need fun or safety,
mutuality or respect,
You might need to be seen, be heard,
you might need to connect.
Creativity? Order? Space or peace?
Tune in, to what your needs are,
Believe me, since I started to do that,
my self-love has come so far.

No longer do I spend my days,
making myself wrong,
It's like I have an alarm bell now,
each feeling is my personal 'Ding Dong!'
Hello, how are you?
What's your message for me?
Are my needs being met or not,
let's tune in and see...

Tune in to my body,
what's actually happening in there?
Do I need to slow down, to breathe,
to show myself some care?
Do I need comfort, or support?
Do I need help right now?
Do I need to state my boundaries
and stop having this same old row?

Do I need to stop doing
all the things for others?
If they make me so tired
I can't lift the covers,

To get out of bed on my only day off,
my energy having all been spent,
On helping others do their things,
I don't know where all the time went?

Self-love is, in essence, about loving you,
enough to make a good choice,
About who you spend time with, what you eat,
drink or don't, and the tone of your inner voice.
Do you speak to yourself in a compassionate way?
Encouraging and cheerleading?
Or do you chastise and shame and blame,
the inner critic you're constantly feeding?

Of course it is different for all of us,
what the acts of self-love really are,
For some it's to sing, paint or dance,
for some it's to play their guitar.
For some it's to spend time in nature each day,
being present and feeling grounded,
And for some it's to look up in history books,
how society's traditions were founded.

So whatever you're feeling,
throughout each day,
Please remember that it's all
completely ok,
You're not broken or tarnished,
or damaged somehow,
You're perfect as you are,
you gotta love you right now.

Even with all the scars and wounds,
and the skills you haven't yet learned,
Your place here on earth is meant to be,
and your love is already earned.
So go for your goals,
your visions, your dreams,
You're allowed to receive them,
to enjoy them in reams.

But to really get there,
you might have to heal,
To allow to the surface
all the things that you feel.
You might need to cry those tears
you buried in the vault,
Or go back to your childhood
to see it wasn't your fault.

And also, find the thing
that makes your heart truly sing,
And then do it every day
until you start to grow wings.

And remember love is infinite,
there is no doubt,
However much you use it,
it can never run out.
So be free, loving others,
keep doing that too,
But make sure you give
a whole lot of love, to YOU!

BECOMING SOBER

I'm here to tell a story,
that feels a bit icky,
And though I know I've got to tell it,
it still feels tricky,
To open up my heart
and share from my soul,
I want to tell you how being sober,
never was my goal.

I never thought
'this drinking lark has gone a bit too far,'
Not even when I found myself drunk,
driving a car.
I never linked together,
how dark my story got,
Because it never felt that bad
until I got out of the rot.
It's only since I've stopped
and shared a few stories from my past,
That I've seen how much I've left behind.
Wow. At last.

No longer am I clouded,
with this sour, drunken haze,
No longer are my nights,
more important than my days.
No longer do I ride the wave
of party after party,
No longer do I see destruction of my body
as somehow, arty.

It sounds a bit serious right? Well it was.

I didn't know why I was drinking,
I did it just because,
Everyone else did it,
my family, my friends,
To me it seemed like the easiest way
to make sure the fun never ends.

I started young, it felt the norm,
to borrow a few sneaky drinks,
Then down the rec to neck the lot
and look real cool me thinks.
I've always been competitive,
never quite knowing when to stop,
'One more? Of course I will, yes please,
fill mine right to the top!'

I learned to believe from quite early on,
that alcohol made you happy.
That having a drink, kept away all the bad stuff,
stopped me from being snappy.
I remember the moment at a party once,
when I decided I liked myself drunk,
I was friendlier, more fun, better, if you like,
when I'd got a few boozy cans sunk.

I then went to Uni, and Oh My Gosh,
I mean, at least I was fully prepared,
For the cheap vodka shots, the buckets of 'Reef'
and the 'stronger' drugs for anyone who dared.

You get the picture,
you know the story well,

Kids and young people,
drunk tales they do tell.
But I didn't stop.
I didn't get a job and settle down,
My partying days weren't over
so I moved to London town.
It's hard to be really honest,
about the next few years,
Because I really did love,
every night with friends saying 'Cheers!'
But the truth is I screwed up big time,
and not just once or twice,
I lost jobs and opportunities
and my bag and phone, more than the roll of a dice.

A boss once told me
I might have a problem, with drink,
I laughed in his face,
how dare he speak what he thinks!
I couldn't hear it then,
I couldn't receive his concern,
I wasn't yet ready
to face the lessons I must learn.

I used to choose my homes
based on their distance from a booze shop,
I chipped my front tooth,
falling off the top of a bus stop.
I missed several flights,
costing me hundreds of pounds,
And I let all my dreams,
fall, to the ground.

I was scared of who I was,
the real me.
I allowed myself to hide,
my authenticity.
I was numbing all the sadness,
all emotions, all the pain,
I believed that I could only handle sunshine,
not rain.
I didn't think I was good enough
to cope with my true being,
I didn't think I was worthy of love,
so chose partners who were fleeing.
I never let myself go for my dreams,
so I never had to face them all failing,
I just lived in my shadow, not in my light,
ignoring the inner wailing.

The booze was so good at numbing it all,
any fear or rejection,
So now I have to work on healing myself,
and stop all that projection.
It's such a deep process
letting go of that mask,
The layers I added
over years from the cider cask.

But like I said before,
it wasn't a conscious thought,
To let go of the booze,
almost by surprise I was caught.
I got pregnant with my son
and that was the catalyst for me,

Luckily I made the decision to stop drinking,
so that he,
Would have a good start in life,
be healthy first of all,
And I wanted to be a good mum to him,
watch him catch his first ball.

But I did keep trying
to start drinking again,
At Christmas and birthdays,
and holidays, and then,
Gradually I realised
it was no longer for me,
It wasn't allowing
my true self to be free.

My body was telling me,
loud and clear,
'Stop doing this Abbi,
you don't need to drink beer,
Check in with yourself, how do you actually feel,
When you consume alcohol?
What is happening? What's real?'

And the answers I found
as I delved deep inside,
Were that I needed to feel everything,
not numb and hide.
But there was a real block
thinking I couldn't be fun,
Unless I'd been drinking,
even just the one.

It took a fair bit of work

on myself to believe,
That I was fun anyway,
good enough to receive,
The highs of life,
the good times, the JOY!
I didn't need any stimulant!
Wow, what FREEDOM! Oh boy!

I'm so grateful to now feel
so strong in my choice,
And now I'm feeling called
to share my story, my voice.

I'm not here to preach
or tell you to stop drinking,
But if you're in any way 'sober curious',
if you've started thinking,
It doesn't feel good
in your life any more,
I invite you to take a walk
through the more conscious door.

Where people like to party
without falling on their face,
And where the venues for dancing,
have a bit more space!
Where you'll feel safe and supported
to let go and release,
Where you can dance in your joys
and claim back your inner peace.

POWER

What does it mean
to stand in my power?
It means to stand strong
and no longer cower,
To the fears and the worries
that run through my head.
I no longer, around others,
have to – softly tread,
In case I upset them
or invoke their reaction,
It's believing I'm safe,
to allow my ideas to gain traction.

My ideas, yes mine,
not yours or theirs.
It's about believing in ME
and saying 'Who cares,
what anyone else thinks?'
Not hearing their doubts,
It's allowing myself the space
to figure it out.

Seeking approval
from parents, teachers and friends,
Would lead me to let go of my dreams,
they'd just end.
I'd feel that wall of negativity,
a crushing blow,
As I asked them their thoughts,
and they said 'No.'
But why was I asking?
Why did it matter?
Why were their opinions

so much fatter,
And bigger and better
and more important than mine?
Why did I let their worries and projections –
dull my shine?

Well I guess,
though it feels weird to admit it now,
I was scared by my dreams
when I didn't know how,
To achieve them, to plan them,
to make them all real,
So I let other's fears,
take over the deal.
I allowed them to stop me,
to put my ideas on hold,
I let my bubbling pan of excitement,
turn, really cold.

Giving my power away to others,
felt like a fair pay off,
So I didn't have to be vulnerable
and listen to them scoff.
I thought it was easier
to push my ideas aside,
Than to say "thanks for your thoughts,
but they can't stop this ride."
I thought other people somehow knew –
more than me,
That by following their way,
perhaps I'd be free.
But no, for so long
I felt restricted and shackled,

I really believed that my dreams,
couldn't be tackled.
I doubted myself so often,
never seeing my worth,
Never realising how deserving I am
of my place here on earth.

I guess I fell into
the hierarchical trap,
Of believing some lives are worth more than others,
wow, what a slap,
In the face of humanity
that is right there?
I'd been conditioned to play victim and cry
'It's not fair!'

Sometimes we get scared when we hear the word power,
we see it as something bad,
Where people abuse it, have control over others
and ultimately it makes people sad.

For me what came next
was to take back responsibility,
To realise that I have the power
to create what I want to see.
If something's not working out,
then rather than blame,
I've started to see,
the whole thing as a game.

Oh interesting that spanner
should appear right now,
On the surface it seems a curve ball,

but I wonder how,
It will actually present
as something perfect on this path?
Like the shower is broken
so I have to relax in the bath.
Or that new job said "No"
and instead of crying,
I know a better one's coming
and just keep on trying.

The power is within me,
to make this life ace,
As long as I take opportunities
appearing all over the place.
As long as I'm open and willing
to look with fresh eyes,
There will always be moments
of delightful surprise.
As long as I see
that it is in my power to choose,
Whether I view each challenge
as something to win, or to lose.
And the only way to lose
is by feeling hard done by,
To win,
I just receive it as a lesson to help my wings fly.

Standing in my power,
standing in my truth,
Being brave, believing in me,
then celebrating, raising the roof!
I am enough. I am loveable.
Even when I get things wrong.

And, my needs are just as important as others
and by meeting them, I feel strong.

True power for me is oh so freeing.
It's about realising that life is what I make it.
I might as well go after what I really do want,
there's no point trying to fake it,
And live for a dream that isn't my own,
or one that's been tarnished by fears.
I allow myself to believe in my own abilities
and follow through on my ideas.

The power in each moment lies within my thoughts,
and repeated they turn to beliefs,
So to be truly powerful, I check in with my mind
and allow myself plenty of relief.

We are all powerful,
all of us here.
Please remember that often,
let go of the fear.
Let go of the bars
you've allowed to be built,
Let your love and creativity pour out,
to be spilt,
From the most powerful bit of you,
the loving part,
Your power comes from your glowing,
and open
heart.

REBELLION

Rebellion is such a powerful
and fascinating word,
It conjures up all sorts of ideas,
every time it's heard.
Ideas of naughty school kids,
ideas of revolution,
Ideas of people fighting back,
of seeking a new solution.

Rebellion is basically,
not doing what you're told,
Even if it's likely
that somebody will scold.
It might be causing destruction,
or damage without a care,
Or breaking the rules and traditions,
when they don't seem fair.

Walking off the beaten track,
going against the grain,
Choosing to ride your bicycle
instead of the crowded train.
It can feel big and unified,
like an uprising or defiance,
Or it can be small and personal
where intimately you pledge your alliance,
To all the values that are true to you,
like freedom, respect and choice.
Sometimes rebellion is speaking out,
reminding people they have a voice.

Remembering that the rules and laws

are not always just and right,
Sometimes we need to stand up and rebel,
sometimes we need to fight.

To rebel we need to let go of the fear,
that we possibly might get caught.
But also we need to take small steps,
to talk and share and support,
Resting when everyone else is busy,
questioning the media,
Sometimes small acts of rebellion,
create real change much speedier,
Than protests, wars and battles fought,
but perhaps we need to use,
Our energy to create the world we want,
it's up to us to choose.

Rebellion could simply be the act
of doing things your own way,
Of following your heart, your gut,
and checking in every day.
To see what feels right for you
and what doesn't feel aligned.
You're a sovereign being, you have the right,
of your own path to find.

If you want my thoughts
on the ultimate rebellion,
Then really it's very simple:
Just don't put the telly on!

THE ILLUSION OF TIME

Tick tock, tick tock,
no longer we hear the seconds.
We get our time now through digits and screens,
their promise of time is what beckons.
We pick up our phones
to check what it is,
Then realise we got distracted
by some other shizz.

We pick it up again,
laughing out loud,
Ok this time I'm checking,
nothing else is allowed,
It's later than I thought,
what have I been doing?
Have I been productive,
or scrolling Insta and cooing?

Some cultures believe that time has different speeds,
depending on the time of day,
Where you get more done at 6am
because time slows out of your way.
And the sleep that you get before midnight,
is more restorative than that you get after,
And of course time flies when you're having fun,
and enjoying all the laughter.

How many of us believe there's not enough time,
to do all the things we love?
We believe somehow it's all the boring stuff
that in the to-do list must come above.
Why exactly is that the case?

Who made those accepted rules?
How come we've let time run the show
and take us all for fools?
Why do we prioritise what isn't important?
The stuff that 'should' get done,
And why do we ignore what we really do want,
the stuff that feels like fun?

We spend time, like a currency,
paying out for chores,
Rather than making time or creating it,
and seeing what's behind those doors
Of opportunity, of wonder,
of brand new chances to take,
'Oh I can't possibly follow my dreams,
I've got packed lunches to make!'

So where does it come from this notion of time?
These measurable moments in a sequence?
It started with the sun and the moon and their cycles,
has it changed a lot ever since?

The clock was developed
to keep accurate time,
And keep people working,
every hour you hear a chime.
Throughout the day you are reminded
where you need to be,
And at the end of the working bit,
a chime says 'You're free.'

There were bells and sounds
to call you in each day,

And to enforce the idea
that you're not here to play.
I've heard it said
that a watch is so called,
Because it took the place of the slave master
in days of old,
No longer does the bell toll
to let us know the hour,
We can keep a check on ourselves,
and relinquish all our power.
Maybe that's too far,
maybe too much,
But what is your relationship with time?
Could it be just as such?

'You don't have time,
time has you,'
I've heard, quite often,
from more than a few.
'Time is money,'
'Don't waste your time on him,'
So much of our lives are spent worrying
that our time might be slim.

If we believe there's not enough,
will we waste what we have away?
If we believe we can create time,
then the game we can start to play.
If we believe time is finite,
that even, it's running out,
Do we allow all the fears to stop us?
Do we listen to the doubt?

But if we really want to LIVE
this one precious life,
Filled with magic and wonder
and joys and no strife,
Then become your own master,
create the time that you need;
Because time comes from within you,
that's the idea I choose to feed.
That I can create time,
and the life that I dream of,
There's no point in waiting for someone else
to tell you what you're made of.

Don't wait for permission,
from outside of you,
Be the creator
of what you want to be true.
Regretting that you've wasted time
is wasting more and more,
So wipe the slate clean
and start doing what you want to live for.

RETURNING HOME

Returning home feels
like I'm going back in time,
I feel like I'm entering
an old paradigm.
Same places, same buildings,
same trees line the way,
Old memories keep surfacing
like they're here to stay.

But the people are different.
They're older, maybe wiser.
There's a new batch of school kids
who've become the early risers,
To walk along the road
to the old brick bus stop,
Where I have memories of teen crushes
and 90s singers of pop.

I run past the fields
where I used to play,
And create new adventures
with my friends every day.
I go past the school
where we helped to dig a pond,
Remembering the hedges we sat in
as we planned to abscond.
We packed our Happy Shopper sweet bags,
full of foraged goods,
As we planned to leave home
and live in the woods.

I remember the apples
that bumped on teachers' cars,

The playground where I fell,
the smell of Dettol cleaning scars.
I feel like I'm pulled back
to former versions of me,
Where somehow my current self
can't be, fully free.
There are memories of struggles
and wounds of the past,
All tangled in together,
holding my body, stuck fast.
I felt called to run,
from the old patterns I fled,
And as I did so I created new memories,
and cleared my head.

As I ran through the woods,
the leaves were falling down like tears,
Shedding layers of the stuff
I'd been holding on to for years.
The old stories were fading
with each step that I took,
Helping me to move on
to a new chapter in my book.

'IT'S SAFE TO LET GO! I shouted.
Enough is really enough.
Those judgements and expectations of mine,
are making everything feel tough.
There's such a process of forgiving,
allowing and moving on,
Accepting that former versions of ourselves,
are now gone.

I'm no longer a teenager
filled with angst and rage,
And my parents have turned over,
a blank new page.
We don't have to live
in the past any more,
It's not helpful for any of us
to be 'keeping the score'.

The only way forward
is with the present moment alive,
To fill it with new memories
and activities where we thrive,
Like singing and dancing
and laughing out loud.
And sharing our celebrations
where we can all feel proud,
Of each other and ourselves
and the journey we've been on.
Like the layers of a Russian doll,
they just keep going on and on.

And what do we get to,
deep inside?
Our own inner child,
eyes open wide.
So let's remember we all have our child selves,
deep within us,
But they're not in the driving seat,
they're a passenger on the bus.

So we can each of us say,
'I'm taking full responsibility.'

And accept that we all need
to set personal boundaries.
And often that is the most
loving thing we can do,
It's actually a way of saying
'I love you,'
enough to want to keep you,
in my life, moving on.'
And respecting each other
is what will make our relationship strong.

We don't need to take
everything so personally,
And if we can own all our triggers,
we'll really be free!
So often, the way through it,
is actually to go within,
And identify those triggers
that keep us caught in a spin.
Work out what's going on
with our own feelings and needs,
And what are those core beliefs
deeply planted like seeds.
Which ones do we need
to pull out at the roots,
And replace with more helpful ones
from which we'll pick fruits?

If we keep telling old stories
of life being hard,
Or we hang on to playing
the 'victim' card,
Then we'll never quite see

all the beauty around,
As the trees start to blossom
and fruits fall to the ground.

So let's embark on a new,
adventure together,
Set foot, all as equals,
to march through the heather,
And the ferns and the meadows,
the rich tapestry of earth.
And let's remember, our past,
does not change our worth.

We are all of us worthy,
whatever we've done,
So let's let go of the past
and choose to have fun!
Let's choose to see the brilliant
aspects of each other,
And celebrate what we've got
as daughter, father and mother.

GRATITUDE

I am grateful for the morning peace,
I am grateful for my home.
I'm grateful for breath to release,
I'm grateful for fields to roam.

I'm grateful for my children,
their kisses and their cuddles,
I'm grateful they remind me,
of the delights of muddy puddles.
I'm grateful for time spent
in the moment while we play,
I'm grateful for the birdsong
that stirs my heart every day.

I'm grateful for my hands
and all that they can do,
I'm grateful for my intuition
guiding me towards what is true.
I'm grateful for the kindness
of a neighbour lending me a pound,
For a trolley while at Lidl,
when my own coin couldn't be found!

I'm grateful for my knowledge
of what foods are good for me,
I'm grateful for my culinary skills
to prepare a delicious and healthy tea.
I'm grateful for the sun,
that rises every morn,
I'm grateful for a stranger's smile
when I am feeling forlorn.

I'm grateful for the abundance,

in apples from our allotment,
I'm grateful for all the natural beauty,
in my local environment.

I'm grateful for all my triggers!
The things that make me shout,
Because they give me the perfect opportunities
to figure a few things out.
I'm grateful for my husband
and how great we are as a team,
I'm grateful for the way we can
support each other's dreams.

I'm grateful for my pencil
that helps me write these words,
I'm grateful for my typing skills,
though as a teenager it felt absurd,
To be learning to be a secretary
(as all of the exercises said)
I remember thinking at the time,
I wouldn't be seen dead,
As somebody else's secretary,
their sidekick, their PA,
But I'm grateful now I can assist myself,
to type all the words I wish to say.

I'm grateful for my mentors,
and teachers and spirit guides,
I'm grateful for all the playgrounds,
tree houses, and slides!

I'm grateful for all the music,
the dancing and the fun.

I'm grateful for all the energy
that comes from that beautiful sun.

I'm grateful for all the flowers,
the colourful and the scented,
I'm grateful for the time to stop and smell,
ALL the roses that are presented.
I'm grateful for friendships near and far,
the new ones and the old.
I'm grateful for the gloriousness
of wood fires that keep me from feeling cold.

I'm grateful for freedom,
I'm grateful for choice,
I'm grateful for so many things
in my life to rejoice.
I'm grateful for swimming
in cold, wild rivers,
I'm grateful for soup to warm me up
after feeling the shivers.

I'm grateful for this day,
the only one of its kind,
I'm grateful for this time,
to myself, remind,
That it's precious, today,
and I'm lucky to be here,
So for that I'm going to celebrate,
go on join me, let's cheer!
Let's cheer for the good times,
the sad times, for them all,
Let's live our lives in gratitude
for all the things, big and small.

FEAR

Allow me to tell you
about a little word called fear.
Though it's so small,
it has a very grand idea,
Of how much it can impact
the life that you lead,
It can feel so powerful,
like a charging stampede.
It can stop you in your tracks,
make you freeze on the spot,
Fear can make you forget
about all the skills that you've got.
But let's strip it back,
let's call it out,
Let's look at what fear
is really all about.

So back in the day
when predators ran free,
Fear helped you by offering
a basic choice of three,
Main ways to deal
with any trouble or attack,
Number one was to fight,
hackles raised on your back
Next one was to run,
take 'flight' to the trees,
And the third was to stop you still,
to freeze.

And sure, these can serve you
if a lion or a bear,
Is there in the woods

with young cubs in the lair.
But these days quite often,
there isn't such a threat,
But those physiological changes,
our body's yet to forget.
These days fear will come knocking,
softly on your door,
And it'll keep coming back stronger
until eventually you can't ignore,
It's message and it's test for you,
so it really is key,
To welcome it in and ask
'what are you trying to tell me?'

We sometimes feel fearful,
about what others think,
I used to quash that down,
by having a boozy drink.
That judgement that we worry over,
the 'oh what will they say?'
It's often just our own perspective
getting in the way.
It's often judgement that we hold
about our own self really,
And even if others do look down on us,
why do we care so dearly?
Why do we need to seek
such external validation?
Perhaps because we have a need
for more joyful celebration?

It doesn't matter what others think,
they're usually just a reflection,

Of your own inner critical thoughts,
striving for perfection.
Perfection that doesn't exist of course,
but that's also masking too,
It's masking the fear you have,
that others won't like or love you.
I used to fear getting things wrong,
and still do on some level.

But that fear's not mine, it's handed down
and I no longer let it revel,
In the success of keeping me stay small,
of not living out my story,
I now take steps to conquer fear
and step up to feel the glory,
Of life beyond the comfort zone,
where magic and dreams run freely,
It's not that scary after all,
once you get past the heebie-jeebies!

There is of course another fear,
that hides out in the rough,
It's buried deep but many share,
the fear of not being good enough.
I haven't met a person yet
that doesn't sometimes feel,
That everyone else is doing better,
that comparanoia, it's there to steal,
The joy, the fun, the ability,
to get totally in the zone,
Remember that their path is theirs
and yours is yours alone.

So own it, claim it, feel your worth,
keep taking steps and moving,
Forward to your dreams and goals,
you deserve them,
YOU'RE AMAZING!

LOVE

When you hear the word 'Love', what do you feel?
Do you come alive from your head to your heal?
Does your heart start to flutter? Your cheeks start to glow?
Or does every sensation begin to slow?
Does it slow to a soft and gentle pace,
Reminding you that life is not a race?
Does it make you stop and look and listen,
And notice the dew drops as they glisten?

Does it make you smell the sweetest of flowers,
And let you to gaze into eyes, for hours and hours?
Does it make you look up and watch the stars,
And marvel at space and, 'is there life on Mars?'

Love is such a precious thing,
Without it there'd be no reason to sing.
Without love there'd be no skip in your feet,
No twinkling eyes, no dancing beat.

You see love is what makes the world keep going,
It's the oil in the cogs, the energy flowing.
It's the lightness, the smiles, the belief and the cheer,
Love is the strong arm holding, the hand of fear.

If you want to know love you can close your eyes,
And listen to the whispers from deep inside.
It nudges and pushes and guides you towards,
All of your dreams, but not on huge bill boards.

You've got to tune in, to listen, to trust,
Only then can you really know what's a must.
For your unique journey, your path, your quest,
Love is your guide towards all that is blessed.

A little bit about me

I've always loved words. Though I didn't always realise how important they were to me. Any business idea I've ever had I've always spent far more time thinking about what it would be called, rather than the business idea itself. And I've always been drawn to words in songs, art, graffiti, posters etc.

I loved to write when I was younger. I didn't know how healing it was at the time. I just knew I had to write. I used to 'journal' long before I'd ever heard of that idea. When I felt angry or scared or confused or anxious, I would write. As a teenager, in my 20s, there was so much writing done in an attempt to unravel what I was experiencing. I wrote poems, loads of them. Angry ones, sorrowful ones, those that were filled with love or fear or angst, or rage.

In love at aged 17, I learned about Haiku poetry and read poems by e.e. cummings, Emily Dickinson and Wendy Cope. I loved them. I used to write on an old typewriter and spent many days getting into a muddle over ink reels and spelling mistakes. Sometimes I wish I'd kept them all. I think I did try to and put them all on a red floppy disc somewhere! Lost, long ago. I do have a few poems and I can still feel the emotions as I read them.

I have notebooks from travelling too. They helped so much. Alone in unknown places and unfamiliar surroundings, it was like confiding into the pages of a long lost friend. There's something magical about writing with no desire to share the words. Like a diary I guess, or a memoir. You can be really true. Honest and raw. It's a helpful process to understand feelings. Still now, when I'm triggered and activated, if I write through it, I can usually get to the bottom of what's going on. Quite incredible really.

I’ve always loved to rhyme. Since I first heard of limericks, I loved to write into the constrained pattern of them. The short, sweet and humorous rhymes seemed friendly, easy and fun. When people left places where I worked, I’d always try to write a limerick in their leaving card. It felt nice, personal.

I’ve always been drawn to lyrics in songs too. Powerful ones, meaningful ones full of passion and protest. I remember listening to the band the Levellers aged about 13 and falling in love with them. They became my favourite band in the 90s. They stood up for so much that I believed in. This line from 'Sell out' really stuck with me. I knew from then that it was important to speak your own truth. And, that it might get you in trouble.

"The year is 1991, it seems that freedom's dead and gone
The power of the rich is held by few
Keep the young ones paralysed, educated by your lies
Keep the old ones happy with the news
Tell the singer not to sing this song
TELL THE POET THAT SHE'S WRONG
And in the courts you'll win the case with lies
Cos you sold them down the river-o"

I went to Glastonbury festival a few times and was awe struck by the poets sharing their words, beliefs and truth, through poetry. And then I think I just forgot it all. I let go of writing and doubted my own voice.

I feel like I’ve always loved to speak or perform, though as a very young child I do remember being ‘shy’. ‘Chatterbox’ was often said of me at school. And if you give me the chance to get up on a stage, I’m there. I love it. Presenting, performing, it feels like part of who I am.

As a teenager I was encouraged not to take drama as a GCSE and it really affected me. I wanted it so bad. If felt like my calling.

I joined a local drama group instead. Had the best years there. I even wrote a short play that was received really well. But I thought it was a fluke. I was asked to write something else but I didn't feel I could do it myself so I borrowed lyrics from a friend's song and used that as my starting point. It felt hard to do it this way. It worked out OK but there was a block there to my full belief in myself.

I'm not sure exactly when I had my first alcoholic drink, but it was around this time. Mid teens. I remember being at a post show party for a play, being drunk. As I wrote about in the poem 'Becoming Sober' I remember consciously thinking that I preferred myself drunk. I feel so sad writing that now. So sad for the younger me that really believed that. I believed I was a nicer person when I'd been drinking. That somehow my normal self was horrible. That was a deeply held belief.

I drank for years. A lot. I never really woke up 'needing' a drink, but in the peak years, in my partying days, there weren't many days that went past when I didn't consume any alcohol. I strongly associated 'Fun' with drinking.

When I was pregnant with my son I knew I had to stop. Luckily I found it easy enough. I had moved to a quiet village by then and stopped going out when I found out I was pregnant. I chose to and was lucky enough to have a smooth time breastfeeding, so I stayed off the alcohol for a while. But then I did try it again. And again. And then gradually I realised I just didn't want it any more. It didn't feel good in my body any more. None of it. I didn't like how it changed me. But I needed help.

Drinking had numbed so much of my life that I felt I couldn't face up to. Feelings I couldn't deal with. Parts of me that I'd never dared look at.

After school I went straight to university and studied communications. I found it fascinating and still do. Connection and community are really important to me. I remember being at a nightclub once and meeting a friend of a friend. He asked what I'd done at uni and when I answered 'Communications' he remarked that I was really good at it! It made me laugh. I am good at it. I guess it's taken me a while to fully realise that.

I spent a lot of my uni life learning about the extracurricular activities of working in restaurants and partying and romantic relationships. I did well enough though, I got a 2:1. Just. I remember one audio project, we'd had to present our group work to the rest of the class but our project hadn't saved so we didn't have anything to show. We'd kind of assumed therefore that we wouldn't have to present anything. Ha! How wrong we were. The tutor was quite clear that every group must present their findings.

Luckily the group ahead of us gave us a handout after their presentation, which listed all the things you needed to do to succeed in group work. I literally took that piece of paper, dragging the rest of my team up with me and proceeded to go through the list explaining all of the things that we hadn't done! That was our presentation. Totally winged it. We scraped a pass. But it showed me that I could do it and pull it off, even with no preparation whatsoever.

My tutor was curious about my attitude to study. After a TV presenting session, he'd described me as similar to Mel and Sue, the daytime TV presenters, early in their career at this time. I was mortified. I didn't want to be seen to be like them. Wow. Maybe if I'd have taken that as the compliment it was meant to be, I'd have progressed down that path with a bit more success. In my final report, my tutor said "there are sinkers and swimmers in this world, and Abbi is definitely a swimmer".

After Uni, I headed to London to live with a friend and after a few too many office temping jobs I took a 'serious' job in a bar where people wore suits! Ha! Not quite me, but I made it fun and enjoyed the access to fine wines and ports. For a bit. But then the daily commute to work in an underground bar, plying rich office workers with lunchtime booze, started to drain my life force energy. I knew I had to get out.

I saw an advert on Gumtree for a radio training course and I knew I was destined to be on it. I remember speaking with a friend about how to approach my boss. I felt really anxious about him saying no. I finally plucked up the courage and he agreed to me working an extra day so I could duck out on a Friday afternoon and head to Shadwell, East London to embark on a pivotal path for me. For the next 5 years I made radio shows! I presented on a few community internet stations and had the best time. I even trained to train others in the art of radio production and really found that great community spirit I had been searching for.

I met an amazing friend and we spent several years going to gigs and festivals in London and Europe, interviewing and dancing to our favourite bands and artists. Happy days.

So you see, I've always yearned to share my words. To be speaking out loud. I'm pretty good at listening too.

In 2020, along with many other people in the world, I was catapulted into a deep journey of self-discovery. I'd heard about this 'inner work' but had no clue what it was. Then my prayers were answered and I found Transformational Coaching. I went deep. I uncovered deep rooted beliefs that were affecting and shaping my life. I wanted more joy in my life. More fun. But I really thought I couldn't be fun without drinking!

With the help of my coach, I worked out what I really loved and I started doing more of that. And one of those things was DANCING! As I mention in the poem 'Dancing' I'd forgotten how much I loved it and how it could be so healing. Dancing brought me back to me again, and for that, I am truly grateful. I started dancing more and more, I ran online dance sessions and then started to host my own dance events too.

Over the next year I trained as a transformational coach myself, and developed my skills in listening even further. One of my amazing clients described me as being both really grounded and excited at the same time! It is amazing to witness the changes that happen when people can tune in and open up to possibilities.

For me I was able to get pretty deep and heal a lot. It's not the full answer of course, nothing is. We all need a variety of support and ways to heal.
Some of my favourites are:
Coaching, meditation, movement, dancing, embodiment practices, sharing circles, writing, sound healing, retreats, laughter yoga, reiki, belief coding, being in nature, wild swimming, being with friends, eating healthily, paying attention to my energy and working on my triggers!

I also truly believe that to be at our best spiritually and emotionally, it's important to look at what we consume into our bodies both in what we ingest in food and drink. And in what we consume via media, social media, our environment etc. The mind control programming is real, AND, we have the power to change it.

Words matter. They are hugely important to our lives. The words we speak, hear, read and see all around us. They really are like spells. They programme our subconscious minds, all of the time. When we start to realise the power of them, we can really shift to a life filled with more positivity, more possibilities and ultimately, more joy. I wish that for everyone. A life filled with more joy.

Well, that was supposed to be a short few words to end the book! I could go on but I'll leave it there. I guess if you'd like to read more, you'll have to wait for book 2...

I think what I really wanted to say is that I'm just so so so so grateful to have found this way of expressing myself and sharing and it really feels like at this moment in time, I am 'On the Write Path'!

The End.

Or is it just the beginning...

Journaling Prompts
(Take a leaf out of my book...!)

What is the most fun you've had in the last week?

When was the last time you laughed out loud? and why?

What are you most grateful for in your life right now?

Who is the most inspiring person you've ever met? Why?

What is your favourite colour? What are your favourite things of that colour?

If you had 3 minutes to share your best lessons from life so far, what would you say?

If I had a magic wand, and anything could happen, what would you wish for?

What can you celebrate about your life and yourself right now?

What are you truly grateful for in your life right now?

If you knew you would be completely supported and everything would work out great, what would your life look like?

Ways To Connect

If you've enjoyed this book and are on social media, let's keep in touch!

Abbi Jinks Poet

@abbijinkspoet

@abbijinkspoet

linktr.ee/abbijinks

For performance or workshop bookings or poetry commissions, public speaking, or for anything else, please email...

abbijinks@hotmail.com

You Are
Amazing